THE CONSORTIUM ON CHICAGO SCHOOL RESEARCH:

A NEW MODEL FOR THE ROLE OF RESEARCH

IN SUPPORTING URBAN SCHOOL REFORM

Melissa Roderick, John Q. Easton, and Penny Bender Sebring | February 2009

THE CONSORTIUM ON CHICAGO SCHOOL RESEARCH
AT THE UNIVERSITY OF CHICAGO URBAN EDUCATION INSTITUTE

Acknowledgments

The ideas in this paper spring from many sources, but the paper itself evolved over several stages in the past three years. First, Melissa Roderick presented an early version at the 15th anniversary celebration for CCSR in 2006. Next came a second iteration that Roderick and John Easton presented in 2007 at the Social Science Research Council's Inaugural Conference of the Research Partnership for New York City Schools, an organization modeled on the Consortium's principles and practices. This final version with Penny Bender Sebring incorporates many ideas from an earlier paper on the history and theoretical foundations of the CCSR by Anthony S. Bryk and Sebring.

Along the way, the direction, rationale, and actual work at the CCSR has been shaped by many co-directors, steering committee members, and staff, as well as our partners in the field—teachers, principals, and central office staff. We owe a tremendous intellectual debt to Bryk, the founding director of CCSR. All of the members of the CCSR staff and steering committees past and present have had a significant role in shaping the research and approaches described in this report. We are particularly indebted to our colleagues Elaine Allensworth, Stuart Luppescu, Jenny Nagaoka, and Susan Sporte, who provided feedback on earlier drafts and have contributed substantively to the development of our thinking. Paul Goren of the Spencer Foundation and Henry Webber at Washington University in St. Louis consistently pushed us to define our organizational identity and articulate our unique approach and theory of action. Tracy Dell'Angela helped us move a rough draft into polished prose.

Finally, we are deeply grateful for our partners at Chicago Public Schools—especially senior leaders Arne Duncan and Barbara Eason-Watkins. It is their commitment to school improvement that we strive to inform and accelerate. Their receptivity to the value of data and research has enabled this stimulating and productive partnership to thrive.

Introduction

The Consortium on Chicago School Research (CCSR) at the University of Chicago was founded in 1990, two years after the passage of the Chicago School Reform Act that decentralized governance of the city's public schools. Since then, CCSR has distinguished itself as a unique organization, conducting research of high technical quality that is accessible to practitioners and policy makers and that is used broadly by the school reform community. Most importantly, CCSR is viewed as making important contributions to school reform, both through the findings and implications of specific research studies and more broadly by improving the capacity of the district to use data, build effective strategies, and evaluate progress.

In this report, we argue that CCSR's focus on building capacity for school reform both sets CCSR's role apart from traditional approaches researchers have used to influence policy and practice and also represents a new model for conducting policy-relevant research. We begin with a brief background of CCSR. We then describe how a focus on capacity building has been institutionalized in a specific set of organizational arrangements that allow us to establish coherence across studies, seek broad stakeholder engagement, and make findings accessible. The report characterizes four traditional models that have guided how researchers seek to inform policy development and practice; we then discuss how CCSR's approach differs. We argue that these traditional roles often fall short in one important area—building the capacity of educators and policy makers. We argue further that developing new roles for research is increasingly important in new policy environments that depend significantly on the capacity of teachers and principals to not only respond to incentives and accountability but also to manage decentralized decision making and school improvement efforts.

As an organization, CCSR's approach to the role research plays in policy development emerged over time as researchers responded to the needs created by educational policy shifts; ultimately, we argue, this approach offers a new model. We characterize this new model as one of focusing on building capacity through supporting the search for solutions.[1] To illustrate, we present a case study of CCSR's work on the transition to high school. We then formalize the lessons learned and how we conceptualize the role of research in supporting school reform in new policy environments. This is the theory of action that drives our research agenda. It guides how we conduct research and how we build knowledge and coherence across a variety of studies.

Background of the Consortium on Chicago School Research

CCSR began in the wake of Chicago's decentralization reforms. The Chicago School Reform Act of 1988 devolved substantial resources and authority to local schools. The law established elected local school councils, giving each council the authority to hire and fire its principal and set its own budget and school improvement plans. Principals gained the authority to hire their own teachers, rather than having to accept teachers assigned by the central office. With greater autonomy came substantial discretionary funding through the redirection of Chapter 1 monies to local schools. At that time, the central office was viewed as a bloated, inefficient, and often inept bureaucracy that was at odds with school reform (Bryk, Sebring, Kerbow, Rollow, and Easton, 1998). Given the magnitude of this experiment, the advocates of reform—largely the foundation community and local reform organizations—believed it was important to establish an independent organization that would be charged with conducting independent, objective evaluations of the progress of reform and engaging in research that would assist local schools in developing their own strategies. Because universities seemed like natural partners in this effort, the Chicago Public Schools (CPS) invited local universities to become involved in evaluating the new decentralization.

This new role—to provide a research-based framework (but not a blueprint) for improvement, to provide critical measures of performance and feedback mechanisms to individual schools, and for researchers to engage in the core questions of what it will take to improve performance—has had a significant impact in shaping the work of CCSR and the role of research in the city.

The 1988 School Reform Act began the first of three significant reform periods in Chicago. In 1995, in response to fiscal crises and union strife, the state legislature again intervened and turned over CPS control to the mayor. This act gave the mayor authority to appoint a new Board of Trustees and to appoint a Chief Executive Officer to replace the Superintendent (Bryk, 2003; Hess 1999, 2002). The first CEO, Paul Vallas, brought in fiscal talent, established union peace, and initiated substantial investments in capital improvements. Most importantly, the new CEO and Board of Education again put Chicago on the national map when they adopted high-stakes accountability as the centerpiece of the educational improvement strategy, which ended social promotion in third, sixth, and eighth grades.

Since 2001, after a change in leadership (both the CEO and the Board of Education), a new administration has initiated yet a third wave of reform. This reform has brought a strong focus to teaching and learning, building capacity in the school system by reforming teacher recruitment, hiring, and professional development. This new administration has focused specific attention on high schools and has instituted a more decentralized strategy to support innovation through creating new schools, allowing schools to opt into specific reform strategies, and promoting more choice for students and parents.

The fact that CCSR was created during a time of decentralization significantly shaped the development of our organization. First, in the absence of a strong central district, the primary audiences for research findings were critical actors in reform: new principals, foundations and other organizations supporting change, and the broader civic community. Second, this expanded audience generated a new focus for research: research must speak to the central problem the practitioners and broader community were grappling with—what would it mean to judge the effectiveness of school improvement and create effective schools?

In this context, the challenge for research was to find ways to inform the question about how to judge school improvement by bringing evidence to bear on the problem and providing critical frameworks for understanding the task. Working closely with other research and reform organizations and the school district, CCSR developed a conceptual framework for organizing its research. *The Essential Supports for School Improvement* (Sebring, Allensworth, Bryk, Easton, and Luppescu, 2006) eventually became a centerpiece of local school improvement planning guides. Starting in the early 1990s, CCSR began to survey principals, teachers, and students to measure each school's status on each of those five essential supports and to guide improvement by giving specific feedback on those measures. Surveys have become a core component of CCSR's work; every two years, CCSR surveys principals, teachers, and students in grades six through twelve. Each school that participates in a CCSR survey receives an individual school report that compares its performance to similar schools on these essential supports, allowing them to track progress over time. This new role—to provide a research-based framework (but not a blueprint) for improvement, to provide critical measures of performance and feedback mechanisms to individual schools, and for researchers to engage in the core questions of what it will take to improve performance—has had a significant impact in shaping the work of CCSR and the role of research in the city. CCSR researchers do not just comprise an independent group that does studies on schools and occasionally announces findings. Rather, our studies and products (e.g., individual school reports) are resources that practitioners use to manage their own improvement efforts.

Over time, CCSR has evolved into a more complex organization. We conduct topic-specific studies on problems, such as student mobility or new teacher induction. We engage in evaluation of district-level initiatives, such as new small high schools or the effects of ending social promotion. We support a range of research studies with diverse methodologies. But key to the success of CCSR has been a consistent focus on these initial themes: (1) research must be closely connected over time to the core problems facing practitioners and decision makers; (2) making an impact means researchers must pay careful attention to the process by which people learn, assimilate new information and ideas, internalize that information, and connect it to their own problems of practice; and (3) building capacity requires that the role of the researcher must shift from outside expert to interactive participant in building knowledge of what matters for students' success. In the remainder of the next section, we discuss how these critical themes are reflected in how we conduct research and disseminate findings and how we view the role of research in informing policy and practice.

What Does it Mean to Conduct Research to Build Capacity? The Organizational Arrangements of CCSR

The three themes discussed above are manifest in five critical commitments that guide how CCSR organizes research and communicates the results of research: (1) developing an extensive data archive on CPS, (2) extensive stakeholder engagement and strong ongoing relationships with the district, (3) conducting scientifically rigorous research while making findings broadly accessible, (4) building knowledge of core problems across time and across studies, and (5) an extensive outreach of providing information to the public.

Developing an Extensive Data Archive on CPS to Support the Study of Reform in a Single District

One of the central and most distinctive activities of CCSR is that we seek to build capacity for research by maintaining an extensive data archive on CPS. Based on an ongoing data-sharing agreement with CPS, CCSR has constructed the most encompassing longitudinal data archive on a city's public system in the country. The database contains complete administrative records on all students for every semester since 1991, course transcripts of all high school students since 1992, and elementary and high school achievement test scores of all students since 1987. CCSR also collects personnel files and, more recently, has added data from the National Student Clearinghouse (NSC) on the college enrollment and college diploma attainment of CPS graduates, beginning with the graduating class of 1998.

CCSR's ongoing surveys supplement administrative data with more detailed information collected from students, teachers, and principals. We first surveyed elementary school teachers in 1991, we included principals in 1992, and we added upper grade students and teachers in 1994. Since 1997, we have maintained a biannual cycle of collecting survey responses from students, teachers, and principals about their school experiences, behaviors, practices, and assessment of school and classroom environments. Surveys also collect additional student background data unavailable elsewhere, including home language and parent education. CCSR also supplements administrative data with U.S. Census data that provides additional background information and the context of schools and communities. We have linked each student's home address and each school's address to census block characteristics and to neighborhood crime statistics provided by the Chicago Police Department. These data are all linked by student- and school-specific identification numbers.

We cannot emphasize enough how this compilation and maintenance of the data archive sets CCSR's work apart from traditional research models and, as a result, how it contributes to our impact. In more typical research, an organization or person gets funded to study a problem. The data for that study is collected (e.g., the researcher develops a survey and convinces a set of schools to administer it). The researcher obtains data and conducts the study. The analytic and technical knowledge gained from those activities is then owned by the researcher. Other researchers can try to reproduce the findings by mounting a similar study or, if studying a different problem, can begin anew in trying to obtain data and dealing with the complicated problems of cleaning messy school data sets.

This still happens in the Chicago. Every year, we hear of independent surveys administered to schools by researchers studying, for example, after-school programs, youth development, or teacher practice. And every year, CCSR fills data requests (with CPS approval) for researchers from other universities who are engaged in independent studies. Administrators seldom hear about the results; only rarely do the results end up shaping future work in a school. Researchers collecting data make well-intentioned promises to feed back their results, but that rarely happens because there is no formal process to follow. Another serious problem with these disconnected studies is that other researchers cannot pick up the development of earlier work and build on it.

Maintaining the data archive provides a solution to many of the problems outlined above. It increases the analytic capacity of researchers to study a wide range of issues and respond to new demands. It promotes coherence across research studies and agendas. And, it builds accountability for researchers. The core purpose of the data archive is to facilitate research and ultimately build the analytic capacity of the city to be able to address multiple research questions and bring data and analysis to the problems of school reform. It allows researchers to draw on a generous and expansive set of data, providing wide flexibility to address new questions and expand the potential complexity of the analyses. This stands in stark contrast to the traditional approach of mounting independent studies; even if researchers share their work, the data an individual researcher collects are designed to address only a particular problem and often do not generalize to new problems.

In this way, CCSR plays the role that the U.S. Department of Education has played in increasing the capacity of researchers by investing in large longitudinal studies. The difference is that, because our work is ongoing within one district, our researchers are able to respond to emerging questions and policy shifts and to do so in rigorous ways. For example, when CCSR was established, no one in the reform community would have predicted that within five years the district would engage in a large-scale initiative to end social promotion. Researchers in other districts, who have faced similar dramatic shifts in policy, often must mount expensive studies from scratch and are limited in the ability to understand changes in performance without extensive pre-reform information. Yet our extensive data archive meant that, within one year of the policy implementation, researchers could quickly track changes in retention rates and student test score performance. Longitudinal surveys meant that we could make comparisons (e.g., teacher practices and students' reports of their experiences in school) pre- and post-reform. The availability of these data enabled one of the most extensive studies to date of the effect of ending social promotion.

The data archive also means that CCSR has become a resource for non-researchers to access reliable information. CCSR regularly receives requests from reporters, external evaluators, and smaller independent organizations for assistance in evaluating their own programs. Often this goes beyond simple data requests. CCSR analysts play an important role in helping other researchers, reporters, and program administrators unfamiliar with large data sets talk through their questions about, for example, the data they need and how to interpret results. Thus, CCSR becomes a technical resource for a wide range of institutions throughout the city that would be unavailable if researchers were acting independently.

A second important function of the data archive is that it allows CCSR to build coherence across research studies and institutionalize research findings into ongoing indicators. For example, CCSR's founder, Tony Bryk, has worked with colleagues to develop several survey measures to tap into their framework of relational trust in schools (Bryk and Schneider, 2002; Bryk, Sebring, Allensworth, Luppescu, and Easton, in press). Since the measures are predictive of student achievement and improvements in student achievement, they now live on as core survey indicators. Individual school survey reports benchmark teachers' and principals' reports of trust in their school against comparable schools in the district. Subsequently, these measures of relational trust have been used by CCSR researchers, who are investigating such different initiatives as small schools. As more studies rely on validated measures, the research base becomes cumulative. Thus, each study builds on the previous one even if topics are different. The result is that core indicators contribute to the capacity of researchers, educators, and the district, allowing them to link across studies and create common dialogue across reforms.

Finally, the data archive is a mechanism that promotes broad cooperation and mutual trust between CCSR and CPS. CCSR researchers need to maintain and expand the data system and ensure schools' participation in surveys so they have a strong incentive to be responsive to schools and the district. Similarly, the central administration and the schools that obtain evidence and feedback see the value of the archive, the studies it supports, and the technical expertise of CCSR to address unanticipated questions. Thus, they are willing to continue to provide data and support survey administrations. It is rare to find such mutually reinforcing relationships with reciprocal accountability among individual researchers, schools, and districts.

Extensive Stakeholder Engagement and Strong Ongoing Relationships with the District

Visitors to CCSR often ask: How do we keep the district happy and maintain relationships with key stakeholders when the news is often bad? This is no easy task. However, we have learned that policy makers and the members of the education community can take bad news if they firmly believe that the research is intended to provide critical direction to reform efforts and constructive feedback—rather than argue a particular, perhaps ideological, point of view. More generally, all parties must share a strong foundation of trust. Engaging stakeholders in the design of the research, regularly communicating findings to the district and the larger reform community, and asking for input from stakeholders in the interpretation of findings is critical in building this trust. Our founders were strongly influenced by the central tenet of stakeholder evaluation: that seeking the input of many voices will enhance both the quality and impact of research.

CCSR institutionalizes stakeholder consultation through its Steering Committee. We are formally governed by an administrative oversight committee and managed by an executive director and co-directors who lead major research projects. Although not directly involved in either governance or management, the Steering Committee, which meets six or seven times each school year for two hours, plays a unique and critical advisory role. It is a deliberately multi-partisan and diverse group designed to represent various school reform voices, opinions, and experiences. The Steering Committee is currently made up of 23 members, who represent two distinct classes: institutional members and individual members. Foundation representatives are ex-officio members.

Institutional members (e.g., CPS, Illinois State Board of Education, Chicago Principals and Administrators Association, and Chicago Teachers Union) appoint representatives. Three CPS members traditionally represent the Chief Executive Officer, President of the Board of Education, and Chief Officer for Research Evaluation and Accountability. All other institutional members have one representative on the Steering Committee.

Individual members include researchers, university and civic leaders, and reform advocates from across the city. They are recommended by a nominating committee of the Steering Committee based on their expertise, diversity of opinions, and involvement in school reform. These positions are not allocated by institutional affiliation.

The Steering Committee has five primary tasks: giving input into the research agenda, reviewing research designs, shaping the interpretation of preliminary results, providing feedback on final reports, and assisting with dissemination. Meetings typically focus on a substantive discussion about a study we are proposing to undertake or a review of research findings. CCSR researchers share study designs and/or preliminary data. Steering Committee members raise questions about methods, inferences, alternative interpretations, and policy implications. Before writing reports, researchers present preliminary findings to the Steering Committee to obtain feedback. Later, they distribute the penultimate draft of each report to members for comments. While the Steering Committee is advisory, its input plays an important role in shaping reports, research, and interpretations. Our researchers frequently receive conflicting advice and perspectives on what is and is not useful in a report. Researchers often head back to work after making a presentation to the Steering Committee feeling energized because either they heard an interpretation they had not tested or they were pushed to take a research finding further.

The Steering Committee assists in ensuring that CCSR research is useful and speaks to various needs and voices. However, the purpose of the committee is not simply to get input into the research. Rather, the Steering Committee is also an important way that CCSR seeks to increase the capacity of the city to engage in dialogue over reform. The committee meetings provide one of the few forums in the city where district leadership has the opportunity to engage in regular dialogue with researchers, union representatives, and leaders of reform organizations around core issues of policy and practice. These meetings offer a forum for lively debate by a consistent group of people who are interested in reform. Participants can talk about problems and interpret research findings openly and respectfully, often setting aside their official roles.

This process of engaging the Steering Committee and diverse stakeholders in debate over research is also critical for CCSR in disseminating research findings. Steering Committee members watch each report unfold, reflecting on preliminary findings in a context where they hear other members' interpretations and reactions. After a report is released, Steering Committee members play a vital role in their respective communities by helping others process the findings, understand the value of the research, and consider how the work fits into a larger research effort. In addition, key members of senior district leadership have time to think in advance about the findings and their implications. Members of the reform community also gradually assimilate the findings and begin to think about ways they can use the research in their own work with schools. Thus, by the time a report is released, key findings often are already on the agendas of the engaged organizations. Having been part of the research process, this group of leaders is eager to start moving on the findings and can

> The "no-surprises" policy is not just an administrative nicety. If CCSR research is to inform policy, researchers must pay attention to the tremendous demands on district leadership and the need to give all stakeholders the opportunity to process findings.

talk about them with confidence. Members of the Steering Committee then become champions of our research, often working to deflect criticism of controversial findings and instead translate research findings into policy and practice in positive ways.

This process of early review is equally important for the district. CCSR maintains a "no-surprises" policy. Before a report is released, we hold formal briefings with the CEO, other appropriate district leaders, and members of the Board of Education. Throughout the process, we seek to regularly inform leadership of findings as they develop. We regularly invite specific administrators from CPS who will be influenced by the research findings to Steering Committee meetings so they are aware of and can address specific findings as they develop. For example, when we conducted a study of CPS students' reports of civic engagement, we reached out to CPS administrators and leaders with a special interest in this area, such as the director of service learning. They had the opportunity to respond to the report and received special presentations of research findings (Sporte and Kahne, 2007).

The "no-surprises" policy is not just an administrative nicety. If CCSR research is to inform policy, researchers must pay attention to the tremendous demands on district leadership and the need to give all stakeholders the opportunity to process findings. The public nature of our work means that many individuals, particularly media reporters, approach new research findings as an opportunity to call the district to task, reveal flaws in reform efforts, or pronounce the district's claims of improvements as counterfeit. If managing these reactions was all that district leadership did, there would be little opportunity to process the potential contributions of the research; ultimately this approach would undermine our role. Regular briefings, formal presentation of research findings to key leaders and to departments who are the targets of the research, and the release of penultimate drafts of reports are all mechanisms that allow the district to feel prepared to respond to research results.

Conducting Scientifically Rigorous Research While Making Findings Broadly Accessible

CCSR's commitment to engaging leadership and reformers is premised on the belief that they will find value in and listen to the research. CCSR must pay particular attention to three questions: What makes research findings "believable?" What makes research findings useful to practitioners and policy makers? And, how do decision makers actually use research findings? Carol Weiss and Michael Bucuvalas (1990) asked these questions about the use of research results in a study of mental health institutions. Based on interviews with decision makers and social scientists, they presented simulations and case studies of real research. One of the most important (and, in their minds, surprising) findings was the value that decision makers place on research quality, or what they term the "technical competence of a study" (Weiss and Bucuvalas, 1990, p. 252).[2] Research is "believed to be useable," Weiss and Bucuvalas conclude, when social scientists do what they are best at: think intently about a problem, are rigorous in analysis and interpretation, and are balanced in inquiry.

Founded by researchers with nationally recognized methodological strengths, CCSR brings to bear the best of social science methodology on the problems facing CPS and conducts research of high technical quality. CCSR studies use rigorous methods for estimating school effects—measuring the "value-added" of schools, accounting for selection bias in estimates, and evaluating the effects of policies. Researchers have waded through the technical details of various methods of constructing dropout rates and have weighed their pros and cons. We also developed new methods for measuring classroom practices (mixing quantitative and qualitative data in analysis) and adequately measuring achievement growth. This technical quality is one of the most important components of our work because people believe the work; it is authoritative. As discussed above, this trust is built in part on a foundation of stakeholder engagement. However, much of the trust comes from the quality of the research itself; decision makers and educators believe CCSR will be objective and rigorous, and that we will provide valuable insights. Developing such a track record not only takes time but also requires high standards of internal quality and review.

Technical quality, however, often can interfere with accessibility and often can create barriers to the usefulness of research findings. While educators often want to be on top of new findings in their field, gaining access is difficult. Particularly in quantitative work, by the time articles reach top journals they are presented in such a technical way that results are no longer accessible to the administrators, teachers, and other members of the education community who were the subjects of the research. School administrators do not have the time or inclination to read dry research articles replete with detailed statistical analyses, and they may not have the training to delve into detailed tables of complicated results from statistical models. The publication and review times of journals are so long that research articles are often outdated by the time they are distributed.

One of CCSR's unique characteristics is our ability to translate research findings into publicly accessible reports that are widely disseminated throughout education and reform communities. CCSR staff members spend hours finding ways to give non-researchers access to more technical analysis (e.g., how you might measure value added, what the effect of failing a course might be in shaping graduation after adjusting for differences in student characteristics, or how differences in students' reports of the academic climate of their classrooms are associated with learning gains). This does not mean steering away from the presentation of rigorous analysis or dumbing down the logic behind the approach. Rather, CCSR reports seek to engage non-academics in the problems that lead to more advanced analysis (e.g., how do we find a comparison group to estimate the effect of retention?) and demonstrate how that analysis changes estimates and interpretations (e.g., how estimates of the performance of students in small schools differ if we compare these schools to all CPS schools or adjust estimates accounting for the fact that new small schools serve more disadvantaged students). CCSR reports have illustrated why it is important to move beyond the percentage of students meeting "national norms" on a given test to consider value-added measures in judging schools. Our commitment to multi-method research also enhances accessibility because we are able to validate quantitative findings with qualitative analysis and vice versa, use qualitative analysis to demonstrate and test alternative hypotheses, and make research findings concrete in real examples of how they play out in schools and in the lives of children (Allensworth, Correa, and Ponisciak, 2008; Newmann, Lopez, and Bryk, 1998; Roderick, Nagaoka, Coca, and Moeller, 2008; Smith, 1998; Stevens, 2008). Multi-method investigation not only enhances the rigor and validity of reports but also makes researchers credible in the eyes of practitioners.

Building Knowledge of Core Problems Across Time and Across Studies

Ultimately, research reports take time to read and absorb, even with painstaking efforts to make them accessible. The window of time in which people pay attention to findings of a research study can be very short. Yet, it requires considerable time for educators to grapple with the importance of the findings, their potential implications, and what those implications mean for day-to-day work. CCSR seeks to extend the time that the results research are considered, first by building coherence across studies and second by developing indicators that keep those ideas on the agenda while individualizing those concepts for schools.

First, the release of a report should not be the last word on a research topic; it must be thought of as the first word or the next word. As CCSR takes on projects (e.g., ending social promotion, predictors of freshman year performance, determinants of college access and success, or effects of small schools), we focus on developing a series of reports that releases critical findings over time and focuses attention on the determinants of a problem. Releasing intermediate results early or midway through the research cycle is difficult, especially when the ultimate conclusions are not clear or when reports focus on pieces of a puzzle rather than on the definitive whole. For example, in our recent work on the transition to college, the first report was intended to identify the central patterns in college attendance and the central issues the school system needs to address. One of the central findings of this report was that Latino

CPS students were much less likely to go to a four-year college than other students; this difference could not be explained by their qualifications, aspirations, nativity, or family background. Thus, the first report identified that Latino students seemed to be having more difficulty, but it did not offer an explanation. This finding then provided the basis for a second report, entitled *Potholes on the Road to College*, which filled in many of the gaps in the first report. It is often uncomfortable for researchers to release findings that raise an important question that is left unexplained. But by releasing those findings, researchers can engage educators and policy makers in addressing the question. This then provides the basis for practitioners to understand the importance of the next set of questions and their connection to the larger picture. Indeed, just as researchers learn by piecing together parts of their research, so too does the practice community. If research is to build knowledge and inform policy, it is critically important that researchers engage in long-term study efforts that also engage the education and reform communities in the findings as they develop over time.

Building coherence across studies is particularly important if that research is to build capacity in schools. A key CCSR finding, which we discuss in more detail in the next section, is that effective schools build coherence across programs. Research studies that are independent and unaligned can pull schools in multiple and opposing directions, leading to the "Christmas tree" approach—a term that Tony Bryk used to characterize schools that used many programs but did not pull them together as a coherent whole. Internal coherence, however, is as crucial to us at CCSR as it is in schools. We need to ensure that all our variables and measures are defined consistently across studies, that our rules for which students and schools are included in which analyses are rational and well documented, and that our statistical programming code for common procedures is consistent from one analyst to another. Our primary vehicle for ensuring this consistency is a two-hour meeting called "data group" that our researchers are required to attend each week. These sessions combine professional development and socialization for new staff, maintain accountability and quality control for all staff, and offer an important venue to ensure that our researchers follow the same jointly determined and documented analytic conventions.

A second important mechanism for building coherence, accessibility, and impact is providing individualized products that allow school-based educators to see how research findings play out in their own school. Individualized Survey Reports (ISRs) allow educators to track over time their status on critical indicators of school environment that research has linked to student achievement. By providing ongoing data around core indicators, ISRs bring research findings to the school, extending the window of time that research is relevant and allowing individual schools to chart their own progress. This allows school communities to continually revisit key concepts of improvement and build their own coherent conceptual models. Over the past several years—particularly because of our emerging focus on high schools and the emphasis in Chicago on supporting decentralized innovation—we are developing more real-time data support for schools and customized ISRs around individual topic areas (e.g., freshmen year performance).

An Extensive Outreach to Provide Information to Broader Audiences

As described above, we strive to present research in accessible formats and develop coherent themes across reports on the key factors for improving instruction, school climate, and student performance. Accomplishing this is essential in helping the district grapple with and identify the core problems of reform. Researchers, however, seldom pay attention to the question of how ideas and research findings actually percolate down into decision makers' and practitioners' conceptualizations of problems and lead to changes in behavior or policy. To many researchers, the implications of their specific findings are obvious. They often assume that the details of what it takes to convert research findings into changes in practice are outside their domain. This challenge—how findings work their way into how people think about a problem, their task, and their work—is a complicated one that must be at the center of how research organizations conceptualize and conduct work.

Charles Lindblom is one of the leading thinkers on the question of how social science can contribute to what he calls "social problem solving" (Lindblom and Cohen, 1979; Lindblom, 1990). Lindblom proposes the idea that practitioners, policy makers, and the public are engaged in a process of interactively trying to solve problems as a part of a complex search for knowledge from a variety of sources. Bryk and Sebring (2001) point out that Lindblom's conception of problem solving contains a radical idea. They go on to say:

The proper aim of applied social science is not to find the one best technical solution to a problem (and then advocate for it) but rather to inform the existing competition of ideas and perhaps, extend it some with the best possible evidence that we can collect (p. 10).

Lindblom's work has been instrumental in the development of CCSR. First, in Lindblom's conceptualization, the role of our research is not to provide the technical answers to problems but to provide technical analysis that informs debate around the core "problems" that engage the public and practitioners. Second, Lindblom and, even earlier, Dewey argued that the work of informing practice requires researchers to be in close interactions with practitioners over time, bringing evidence to bear on the debate (Dewey, 1927). A focus on solving problems implies that there will be significant lag time between the release of a study and the effect it might have. The view that research findings and impacts on policy take time and are often indirect is supported by Weiss and Buculavus (1990), who found that specific research studies can seldom be directly linked to changes in practitioners' work (e.g., seldom could policy makers point to a piece of research that directly impacted a decision they made). They found instead that *"the research information and ideas that percolate into their stock of knowledge represent a part of the intellectual capital upon which they draw in the regular course of their work"* (p. 263).

Key to this process is not only changing the relationship between researchers and practitioners but also changing the way practitioners interact around research. Principals, teachers, administrators, and the larger reform community will not be able to take the findings of a CCSR study and immediately put them into practice. Rather, the ideas behind that work need to be heard in multiple ways over time if practitioners are to understand the findings, connect them to problems they face in their own work, and integrate that knowledge into how they do their work in schools. This takes time, and it requires that practitioners interact around findings with researchers and their colleagues.

All of the organizational characteristics and approaches discussed in this section are ways that we explicitly pay attention to the process by which research findings get assimilated into practice. Maintaining the data archive keeps key findings alive in ongoing research. The Steering Committee's engagement creates an opportunity for top school leaders to process ideas and become intermediaries in disseminating findings and developing their implications. Readable public reports provide resources to principals and other administrators that they can use with their staff over time. But a critical final component of our work is our commitment to disseminating research findings through systematic engagement and interaction with educators and the larger reform community. A major CCSR study is likely to be released at a city-wide symposium attended by Steering Committee members and district staff, as well as a broader range of representatives from foundations, reform groups, and the education community. A press conference is planned to follow the symposium. Before both events, we hold pre-release briefings with the Chief Executive Officer, the CEO staff, and Board of Education leaders. In advance, we also brief district staff and representatives from groups of schools that are affected the most by the findings. The public release, however, is often the starting point for a broader engagement of the education community. For example, within several months following the release of our first report on college access, enrollment, and performance of CPS graduates (Roderick et al., 2006), researchers made as many as 20 presentations to district staff, groups of principals, college reform organizations, and the foundation community. For a report on what matters for freshmen performance released in 2007 (Allensworth and Easton, 2007), we created two-page briefs customized for different audiences that summarized key findings about the importance of grades and attendance. The district CEO mailed these briefs, in English and Spanish, to the homes of 55,000 incoming freshman in 2007 and 2008. Versions emailed to principals were widely used for teacher training and freshmen orientation. This public dissemination strategy is not just aimed at getting as many people as possible to hear about findings. Rather, having the opportunity to see researchers present and talk about the work, ask questions, and process the information with peers is critical if the education reform community is to have the opportunity to grapple with what research has found and develop implications for practice.

In this section, we described how CCSR organizes the work to give broad access to research and inform the ongoing dialogue around reform. We have argued that the "how" of the work we do (how we interact with practitioners, organize research, and disseminate findings) includes critical mechanisms that can be used to build capacity within systems. As we have argued, our focus on building capacity requires explicit attention to the process by which we engage practitioners in research. A focus on building capacity also requires developing an explicit theory of action for what role social science research can play in informing school reform that guides the choice of what topics we study and the design of the research. In the next section, we discuss CCSR's emerging theory of action that drives our research agenda and the design of our studies: the "what" (what topics we study) and the "for what" (what role specific research studies can play in shaping reform) that we argue has been critical in shaping CCSR's impact.

Redefining the Role of Research in Informing Policy Development and Practice: Traditional Models and Their Limitations

Each time we are asked, "How has CCSR influenced policy? How do we know that we have had an impact?" the tendency is to cite studies that policy makers have reacted to by changing policy. The series of studies regarding the end of social promotion caused the district to change its criteria for promotion and, several times throughout the study, led to changes in district policy (Nagaoka and Roderick, 2004; Roderick et al., 1999; Roderick et al., 2003). Our 1996 report entitled *Charting Reform in Chicago: The Students Speak* (Sebring et al., 1996) led to a major policy planning process in the district to improve high schools. Funders often evaluate the quality of the work by whether it hit the front page of newspapers and whether there was a "measurable" policy response. In this section, we argue that this traditional way of seeing the role of social scientist—that of external initiator of significant policy changes—represents a paradigm that not only mischaracterizes our approach and impact but also represents an ineffective strategy for building capacity within a school system. We also argue that CCSR's approach has evolved as an alternative to the traditional policy planning model, one that focuses not on initiating policy changes but on encouraging and perhaps catalyzing policy development over time. To make this case, we first step back to look at traditional roles that social scientists have played in influencing education policy and practice. We then contrast the traditional approach of policy planning with a newer approach that we, borrowing from William Easterly's (2006) work in development, term "supporting the search for solutions." We provide a case study based on our research on freshman-year performance to illustrate these differences.

What Roles Have Researchers Traditionally Played in Influencing Educational Practice?

If we think about how university- and college-based educational researchers have sought to influence policy and practice in education over the past several decades, four basic models emerge: (1) creation of the big idea, (2) development and identification of effective model (R&D), (3) external evaluation, and (4) traditional policy analysis.

THE BIG IDEA

A first way that researchers have influenced education practice is through "big ideas" that often seem to offer magic bullets for reforming school systems. In the wake of *A Nation at Risk* (National Commission on Excellence in Education, 1983), big ideas have largely driven education policy. Much of the debate in education policy has been about the efficacy of these ideas. To name just a few, these big ideas include markets and choice, accountability and high stakes testing, standards, merit pay, and decentralization. The originators of the big ideas are less focused on the day-to-day practice

> One of the reasons CCSR has made an impact is because Chicago's reforms (decentralization, accountability, choice) explicitly created markets for ideas and produced significant incentives at the local level for principals, teachers, and external reform organizations to try out different models.... Such incentives are rare in public education.

of teaching and more concerned with identifying which operational and governance models create incentives and conditions for improvements. For example, markets do not create effective schools but create conditions under which institutions have the opportunity and incentives to innovate.

There is no doubt that the big ideas have largely transformed public education in major cities and shaped education policy nationally. One cannot talk about Chicago school reform, No Child Left Behind, or reform in virtually any major school system or state without referring to the big ideas. Decentralization, privatization, accountability and high stakes testing—and now choice and new school development—are the big ideas in Chicago that have driven change in the system.

RESEARCH AND DEVELOPMENT

A second role that researchers play in informing practice is developing clinically based programs and strategies intended to improve instruction and school conditions. Success for All, Reading Recovery, Accelerated Schools, the School Development Model (James Comer), Talent Development High Schools, and First Things First are all well-known examples of models developed by researchers. The strategy for influencing practice through model development is well established: (1) use existing research findings and theory to develop an effective intervention, (2) implement the model and test its effectiveness, (3) replicate the model in different settings and test scalability, and (4) move to rigorous evaluation of impact. The theory of action of such approaches is that practitioners need good models and evidence of effectiveness. By developing what works, we can then build knowledge of effective practice. This research-practice paradigm is largely the approach embodied in the U.S. Department of Education's Institute for Educational Sciences (IES), which explicitly outlines this process in its requests for proposals. The role of the researchers, as described by IES, is to develop models, test their effectiveness, and then test the efficacy of bringing these ideas to scale using rigorous methods.

EXTERNAL EVALUATOR

A third role for research, also reflected in the IES model, is to be "objective and rigorous evaluators of policy." This is often how policy makers view the role of researchers. When we interact with leaders in other school districts about their research needs, invariably they tell us what they need from research is "more help evaluating the programs and policies we have put in place." Evaluation also has become how many quantitative researchers see their role in advancing education policy. Advances in causal modeling and randomized experiments have become an increasingly popular and prestigious domain of education research. The evaluator role in this case is not one of shaping policy or practice but seemingly validating (or not) whether changes in policy or practice work using rigorous causal methods to identify the impact of new initiatives. In many cases, the researcher is less interested in understanding the problems of practice than in developing and testing methodological approaches to conducting rigorous evaluation (e.g., lottery studies, randomized experiments, regression-discontinuity designs, and propensity score methods).

Big idea generation, research, and development of effective practices—as well as the use of research to rigorously evaluate policy—are all important roles. What we have learned over time, however, is that none of these models creates sustained relationships between researchers and districts that builds broader capacity and brings focus to the core processes at work within schools across reforms. Capacity problems are too often the barrier rather than the core focus on many reform efforts. It is a familiar theme in education research that effective models fall short when replicated because of the lack of capacity of educators in the building to adopt reforms and effectively manage implementation. As importantly, one of the most consistent findings in our research in Chicago is that, while the big ideas have had important impacts on schools and often created the conditions for reform, decentralization and accountability also act as sorting mechanisms that stratify schools according to their initial capacity to respond to new initiatives. Because filling this gap has driven the development of the CCSR theory of action and work, we begin by illustrating the central problem that focused CCSR on capacity.

The first two waves of school reform in Chicago were driven by two sets of big ideas: decentralization and accountability. Yet in both cases, the conclusion of CCSR's research was that waves of school reform fell short by not focusing on building the capacity of schools to respond to new policy demands. Our early work on the impact of decentralization in Chicago, for example, concluded that many Chicago schools improved during the first wave of school reform. But by the mid 1990s, it was also clear that a significant group of schools had been left behind. A CCSR report entitled

Charting Reform in Chicago: The Students Speak (Sebring et al., 1996) examined the quality of learning environments in the nearly one-quarter of elementary schools (104) on the state's academic watch list. It found that these poorly performing schools were characterized by weak leadership, a lack of any focus or impetus for school improvement, and extremely weak learning norms among students. These problems had not improved under decentralization (Sebring, Bryk, Roderick, and Camburn, 1996). The report concluded that these schools (which were predominantly African American, overwhelmingly low income, and economically and geographically isolated) had become "organized to maintain the status quo" and lacked the institutional capacity to respond to the incentives and resources provided by decentralization. The report concluded, *"Left to their own devices, it is unclear that many of these elementary schools have the human resources and collective will to improve"* (Sebring et al., 1996, p. 75). Indeed, a subsequent analysis of trends in academic productivity during the early 1990s found that decentralization was associated with widening inequalities in student achievement across schools (Sebring, Allensworth, Bryk, Easton, and Luppescu, 2006).

A similar theme emerged out of other CCSR research on the impact of accountability and high stakes testing. In a study of Chicago's school accountability policies, Finnigan and O'Day (2003) found these same internal conditions—whether schools had strong leadership and high initial measures of "essential supports"—were central predictors of whether schools placed on probation were able to improve rapidly in the first several years of the policy. Similarly, Roderick and her colleagues' evaluation of ending social promotion concluded that high-stakes testing largely sorted students and schools by their capacities to respond to the motivation and incentives created by the policy (Roderick, Nagaoka, and Allensworth, 2005). This was true in predicting which students were able to raise their test scores and be promoted. It was also true in predicting whether schools could effectively use the policy as a focus for organizing their improvement efforts. As Roderick and her colleagues (2005) discussed in their assessment of why learning gains in Summer Bridge (the summer school program mandated for students who did not initially meet the promotional standards) were nearly three times as large in high- versus low-achieving schools:

> *Perhaps the most convincing evidence that capacity mattered came from Summer Bridge. Even with its highly structured approach, students in schools with higher school-year achievement had significantly larger test score gains in Summer Bridge, even after accounting for the fact that schools with low achievement during the school year tended to serve lower-achieving students during Summer Bridge. . . . Given the strength of our summer school results, it is not surprising that retention was as much of a school as a student phenomenon.*

Thus, we concluded that decentralization and accountability initiatives did not build capacity but instead that they were "capacity sorters." This conclusion is also a familiar refrain in research on the effectiveness of scaling up effective programs and many program evaluations. But, the conclusion that indicators of school capacity (i.e., whether schools have strong leadership, professional communities, and strong internal conditions) largely predict whether education reforms (e.g., accountability and implementation of effective models) will work raises a question that is at the core of CCSR's purpose: Is there a role for research in focusing on changing that capacity and moving those core indicators? CCSR is often characterized as a policy analysis organization because of our focus on what matters for student and school improvement. Yet, as we will argue, the traditional policy analysis role also has serious limitations that have challenged us to rethink the role of research in supporting policy development.

TRADITIONAL POLICY ANALYSIS

The traditional role of policy analysis organizations is to provide expert advice to the public sector devoid of political influence and interest-group politics. Carol Weiss has done substantial work on the history and development of policy analysis as a field and on the formal organizations that support such work. (We refer readers to her substantive work for the history of this field: Weiss, 1991; Weiss and Bucuvalus, 1980; Wagner, Weiss, Wittrock, and Wollman, 1991). Born in the progressive era and blooming in the post-war era as researchers developed more sophisticated analytic techniques for analyzing social science problems, policy analysis as a field is based on the assumption that better policy could be created with more scientific approaches to both evaluating evidence and alternative decisions. At present, many school districts come into contact with policy analysis models and tools when they commission external consulting firms for specific projects to organize data, bring standard planning techniques to bear on problems, and provide expert support to identify sets of policy options.

Of all the research roles described in this section, policy analysis has come under the strongest critique for over reliance on such mechanistic methodologies as cost-effectiveness and cost-benefit analysis and simplistic consideration of broad-brush policy alternatives (e.g., the costs and benefits of merit-pay versus professional development for teachers) with little attention to detail. These approaches often lead to simplistic answers and "big-plan solutions" that never get fully implemented. Nevertheless, the policy analysis and planning approach is what we would characterize as the predominant paradigm used by researchers and the foundation community in conceptualizing how research findings should shape policy. To simplify how research impacts policy in this conceptual approach: (1) the policy maker or researcher identifies a problem (school dropout); (2) the researcher or policy analyst conducts a series of analyses and presents findings; and (3) policy actors react, create a plan to fix the problem, and then implement it. This approach has all the limitations of other top-down solutions that do little to build the capacity of the school professionals, who are then charged with implementing the plan to understand the nature of the problem and why the chosen solution is better than other options. Neither does this approach engage local actors in designing the implementation of solutions. Ultimately, externally imposed solutions become unfunded and unsupported.

Having experienced the limitations of this approach, we argue that effectively creating new models of research requires a fundamental rethinking of this fourth approach to the role of research. Indeed, it was the experience of CCSR researchers with the failures of a traditional policy planning approaches and our shift in approach over time that allowed us to turn a major failure into a success.

The Transition to High School in Chicago: A Case Study of CCSR's High School Research as an Illustration of the Development of CCSR's Theory of Action

Our 1996 study entitled *Charting Reform in Chicago: The Students Speak* provided a very negative assessment of CPS high schools, describing them as a "case of institutional failure" (Sebring et al., p. 78). The research highlighted the difficulties students in Chicago were facing in the transition to high school. It documented that high rates of failure in ninth grade, even among students with adequate entering skills, led to a spiral of failure and disengagement. The report received wide media and policy attention and established CCSR as a critical player in the new "mayoral takeover" reform era, moving us from an organization seen as aligned with the decentralization reforms to one that could inform new policy development and reform efforts. The report's findings caught the attention of the newly appointed Chief Executive Officer, Paul Vallas.

The response of the administration followed the traditional policy-planning approach and would be seen as one of the most substantial impacts CCSR had on policy. Vallas began a large-scale planning process organized around a series of planning committees. The resultant document, entitled *Designs for High Schools*, adopted as its organizing principles our terms "academic press" and "personalism." *Designs for High Schools* was adopted by the Reform Board of Trustees in March 1997. In a bold move, the CPS Board of Education raised high school graduation requirements so that all students would take a college preparatory curriculum aligned with admission requirements of local four-year universities. End-of-course exams would ensure that courses would be aligned across high schools. The plan provided for increased support for students through mandated academic advisory periods and new freshman academies.

Instead of buying into the new mandates, most high schools resisted efforts toward restructuring their curricula. The initiative experienced all of the pitfalls of the policy planning approach. Most of the reform efforts, with the exception of changes in graduation requirements, fell short. Teachers and the union strongly resisted mandated advisory periods and the end-of-course exams. Union pressure resulted in advisory periods becoming optional at each school. The initiative was inadequately funded, so that promised advisory curriculums and supports did not emerge. End-of-course exams, which were initially required and were to be a substantial portion of a student's grade, never made it out of the pilot phase. Widely criticized for their poor quality, the exams were eventually discontinued. In the end, predictably, evaluators concluded that the reforms were a failure because they were badly implemented, unfunded, and resisted by teachers and principals (Hess and Cytrynbaum, 2002). Looking at high school trends, CCSR researchers Shazia Miller, Elaine Allensworth, and Julie

Kochanek (2002) concluded that most improvements in high schools between 1993 and 2000 could be attributed to improvements in the elementary schools because so many more students were entering high schools with higher skills. Recent analyses of these reforms, moreover, found little evidence that the increase in high school graduation requirements led to improved student performance (Allensworth, Nomi, Montgomery, and Lee, 2007).

From the Front Page to the Principal's Desk: "Organized for Failure" to "On-Track for Graduation"

To those familiar with CCSR's research on high schools, particularly on the ninth grade, it may seem odd to characterize our earlier research in this area as a "failure." There are few high school principals in Chicago today who would not highlight improving freshman-year performance as a central focus of their reform efforts. Indeed, CCSR studies on the importance of freshman year have had national policy significance (Allensworth and Easton, 2005; Allensworth and Easton, 2007). But that influence did not emerge from the initial studies. It emerged later as CCSR researchers interacted with policy makers and educators around the central problems in the ninth grade transition experience. This story illustrates, for us, the critical lessons we have learned about the role of research in building capacity in urban school districts.

In the late 1990s, as the high school reforms described above were struggling, our researchers developed a way to report to elementary schools how their eighth grade graduates fared in high school. Influenced by Roderick and Camburn's (1996, 1999) work on the impact of course failure in ninth grade, another group of our researchers sought to measure the success of elementary school graduates in their transition to high school. The result was a quantitative indicator that assessed whether freshmen were "on-track" to graduate. Students were on-track if they had completed enough credits by the end of ninth grade to be promoted to tenth grade and had failed no more than one semester of a core subject. These indicators were incorporated in a series of CCSR reports that showed improving trends during freshman year on this critical variable predicted high school graduation (Miller et al., 2002).

On the strength of this research, the new CEO, Arne Duncan, adopted the on-track indicator as an additional criterion for evaluating high school performance. He was responding to criticism from principals that they were being judged solely on the basis of annual standardized test results. Principals argued that simplistic test score criteria did not reflect whether they were moving students forward and, in particular, whether they were succeeding in engaging more students and reducing dropout rates. Chicago's charter schools already were being evaluated on broader measures of performance and had used freshman-year outcomes as one of their indicators of school success. On the basis of the positive reaction to that policy, Duncan settled on new criteria for judging high schools that included test scores, dropout rates, and the percentage of ninth graders who were on-track. Schools were judged on both their status on these indicators and on their improvements over time.

Adopting the on-track indicator as an accountability measure would seem a simple addition with straightforward implications: hold schools accountable for their on-track rates, which is a leading indicator for high school graduation rate, and they will work on the problem. It was clear, however, that schools did not fully grasp the connection between being on-track in the freshman year and later graduation. In 2005, CCSR researchers briefed central office leaders and all high school principals on the findings of a major report on graduation and dropout trends. Principals responded that they lacked sufficient information to fully understand the dropout problem in their schools, develop interventions, and monitor their success. CCSR researchers Elaine Allensworth and John Easton decided that it was important to return to the initial findings that generated the on-track indicator. They updated their analysis and released a short report that clearly defined the on-track indicator and demonstrated its relationship to high school graduation (Allensworth and Easton, 2005). The simple findings of the report ("students who are on-track are four times more likely to graduate than students who are off-track") established for schools and the reform community the close connection between being on-track and graduating, lending greater urgency to improving the freshman-year experience and intervening with struggling ninth graders.

The on-track indicator, defined and validated in a simple report, has become an important lever for coherence among high school reform efforts in Chicago. New high schools and new reform initiatives, such as the Gates High School Transformation Initiative, have adopted improved freshman-year performance and "the proportion of students on-track to graduate" as a central focus of their efforts and indicator of success. The freshman-year experience, we would argue, is now seen by educators themselves as a key problem to solve, and they are searching for external supports and guidance in finding solutions. Recently, CCSR released a follow-up report, entitled *What Matters for Staying On-Track and Graduating in Chicago Public High Schools*, that provided a more detailed analysis of the instructional and school characteristics and the patterns in student behavior that contribute to lower rates of course failure and poor course performance during freshman year (Allensworth and Easton, 2007). That study provided more specific tools for schools so they could move from a focus on the indicator itself to identification and implementation of strategies to improve on-track rates. Educators responded. High schools in the city organized freshman orientations and the opening of school around this report. The CEO, Arne Duncan, sent a letter home to parents of incoming freshman with a brief, user-friendly synopsis of the report.

We present this case to illustrate the stark differences in the role of CCSR research in these two time periods. Our first report on high schools in 1996 and the subsequent policy response could be characterized as following a very traditional policy planning model: An "outside" research organization identifies the big problem ("high schools"), and the administration implements a big-plan process that seeks to identify technical solutions with little attention to whether educators on the ground understand why the mandated solutions matter in their day-to-day work.

As a result, the problem we were trying to solve (high rates of freshman course failure) faded into the background as people argued over the right solution to high school reform. And, as has been the policy tradition, big plans were made with little attention to the details of implementation, with little accountability for whether plans fall short, with little attention to measuring progress and adjusting accordingly. Thus, the role for the evaluators then was to pronounce that the reforms did not work.

Our newer research on the on-track indicator focused on the same set of issues but put the specific problem of students' course performance and high school

Our role was to bring measurement to bear to help educators identify a critical focus for their efforts. The solution to the problem was not prescribed by the research; rather, answers were intended to come from the practitioners. The role of the central office, moreover, was to get schools focused on the problem—ultimately giving schools incentives to innovate, rather than mandate, a singular top-down solution.

graduation front and center. We began working with educators to conceptualize the central problem they were trying to solve—in this case, improving student performance in high school. Our role was to bring measurement to bear to help educators identify a critical focus for their efforts. The solution to the problem was not prescribed by the research; rather, answers were intended to come from the practitioners. The role of the central office, moreover, was to get schools focused on the problem—ultimately giving schools incentives to innovate, rather than mandate, a singular top-down solution. The approach then focused on building consensus around a core issue, finding what was needed and making adjustments accordingly.

How do we characterize this alternative approach? We borrow the term "searching" from William Easterly, formerly of the World Bank. Easterly (2006) issued a virulent critique of the traditional "top-down" policy approach in his recent book entitled *The White Man's Burden: Why the West's Efforts to Aid the Rest Have Done So Much Ill and So Little Good*. Easterly contrasts "Planners" with "Searchers," arguing that development efforts have been dominated by big plans and top-down solutions that assume problems are easy to solve and require simple technical solutions. Big plans result in grandiose objectives that are never realized and for which the initiators of the plan are never held accountable. Easterly argues that development policy would do better not with big plans and top-down solutions but instead by creating conditions so people on the ground are given the incentives, resources, and feedback they need to search for solutions. Giving multiple examples of successful development projects, Easterly argues that, like our case study of the on-track indicator, many successful projects are characterized by practitioners working on pieces of the problem—not knowing the answers in advance but instead finding answers through experimentation and trial and error.

Easterly's critique of the policy development process does not focus on the role of research but the ways in which planners approach policy solutions. This is an important distinction. The key policy question is: How do you create conditions that encourage and even incentivize local actors to search for solutions? We believe that one of the reasons CCSR has made an impact is because Chicago's reforms (e.g., decentralization, accountability, choice) explicitly created markets for ideas and produced significant incentives at the local level for principals, teachers, and external reform organizations to try out different models. Thus, the CCSR model was developed in the context of a policy environment that supported new roles for research by creating incentives for educators to look to research for new ideas and that gave educators the autonomy and often the resources needed for innovation. Such incentives are rare in public education. In writing about the problems of scale, Richard Elmore has noted the following:

> *At any given time, there is an abundance of ideas about how to change the fundamental relationships in the core of schooling…. The problem, then, lies not in the supply of new ideas, but in the demand for them. That is, the primary problem of scale is understanding the conditions under which people working in schools seek new knowledge and actively use it to change the fundamental processes of schooling* (p. 4).

If research is to inform practice, it is critical that the policy environment rewards and incentivizes innovation and new ideas, creating a market for ideas. Thus, it is critical to CCSR's influence that the district engages in reforms that support innovation and incentivize demand for data and research input.

Policy mechanisms that decentralize decision making and produce incentives for change open up an entirely new role for research—one that CCSR embraced from its origins. That new role—what we term supporting the search for solutions—is that research can help fill in a missing and necessary support amidst the big ideas that create conditions for change, the model developers that offer externally developed solutions, and the evaluations that conclude that efforts at reform will ultimately fail without capacity building. Bringing research to bear on enduring problems that practitioners and decision makers confront can provide a focus for efforts, support in identifying effective strategies, and the feedback that is essential for improvement.

How CCSR Carries Out Research to Build Capacity and Advance School Reform

A central tenet of CCSR is that capacity-building research does not seek to provide the answers or promote specific solutions. Rather, we bring to bear the best techniques of social science research on the central issues facing urban schools in ways that help identify: (1) the key indicators for improvement, (2) the frameworks that guide educators on how to connect these indicators to school practices; and (3) the theory of action behind new district-wide policies and how these new policies fare in practice. This requires moving away from siloed studies where researchers work alone and produce disconnected findings to a focus on developing coherence across studies in ways that build the system's and practitioners' capacity to understand outcomes that matter, their role in shaping those outcomes, and more coherent approaches to solving their central problems. In this section, we describe these three main research activities as they play out within and across studies.

INDICATOR DEVELOPMENT: THE CRITICAL ROLE OF MEASUREMENT

Measurement is an integral part of all social science research, but it a particularly critical activity for CCSR. Our attention to measurement distinguishes us as a research organization that goes beyond studying school reform to assisting in the process of improvement. As illustrated in our example of the on-track rate, good measurement brings conceptual clarity by precisely defining the phenomena we are trying to change. Good measurement enables researchers to build frameworks that integrate multiple concepts and help us better understand mechanisms and pathways to improvement. Educators need these frameworks for improvement. What student behaviors (e.g., attendance, homework, or classroom engagement) are associated with increasing the likelihood of students being on-track for graduation? Are the predictors of being on-track freshman year different than the predictors of high GPA? And, what elements of school and classroom environments are associated with student behaviors that lead to improved class performance? Finally, the conceptual clarity brought about by good measurement helps us communicate and develop a common understanding of important issues.

Three examples of the importance of "measurement in action" illustrate these points. First, measurement is about clearly identifying which outcomes matter. This would seem straightforward: raise test scores, increase graduation rates, and get students to enroll in college. But measuring student achievement is not an easy task. For years, researchers have resisted attempts to judge schools simply on average end-of-year test scores. These scores are highly correlated with the students' family background; thus, schools that serve children from disadvantaged families are judged to be bad.

Under Tony Bryk's leadership, one of CCSR's most important projects was an effort to measure academic productivity in CPS elementary schools. He asked: "How much do students learn while they attend school?" and "How much do schools contribute to students' learning growth?" Over several years, we developed a method to judge the "productivity" of CPS schools—work that laid the foundation for our subsequent research to investigate the determinants of that growth. This research on academic productivity ultimately shifted the conversation in Chicago towards improvement and away from a simple normative comparison (Bryk et al., 1998).

Measurement is not about just achievement and attainment outcomes. It is also about defining, testing, and measuring constructs critical to organizing schools for improvement; thus, assisting educators in developing broader frameworks for what matters. In one of our first reports, *A View from the Elementary School*, Bryk and his colleagues described a "Christmas tree" school (Bryk et al., 1993). In this school, the principal used the resources provided by state Title One funds to purchase an indiscriminate range of programs. These programs were compared to the ornaments on a Christmas tree, displaying a great deal of energy and innovative spirit. The problem was that all these new programs were unconnected and uncoordinated; teachers and students alike were adversely affected by this incoherence. In some instances, students moved from a whole-language approach to teaching reading in one grade to a direct-instruction approach in the next grade. The study contrasted the Christmas tree school with a school where the programs were coordinated and aligned both across and within grades—a set of practices that we call program coherence.

The next step was to measure this concept through large-scale survey data collection. In our surveys, we asked teachers a series of questions about the degree to which they

This requires moving away from siloed studies where researchers work alone and produce disconnected findings to a focus on developing coherence across studies in ways that build the system's and practitioners' capacity to understand outcomes that matter.

feel: programs at their school are coordinated with each other and with the school's mission; instructional materials are consistent within and across grades; and there is sustained attention to quality program implementation. Together these items form a highly reliable scale.

This survey measure then was validated by field work in the Chicago Annenberg Research Project (Newman et al., 2001). Based on numerous visits, observations, and interviews, researchers independently rated schools on the degree of program coherence. Most importantly, we have found that schools with high program coherence are more likely to improve student achievement (Sebring et al., 2006); and, similarly, schools that become more coherent over time are more likely to improve student achievement as well. Moving "coherence" from a research finding in one study to a measured concept that could be linked to student achievement and tracked over time was a critical way in which CCSR translated a research finding into validated indicators schools track over time. Careful measurement enabled us to better understand this phenomenon. It helped us understand how various concepts are related to one another (e.g., how leadership affects program coherence) and, therefore, adds to our understanding of school improvement as a phenomenon.

SUPPORT IN IDENTIFYING STRATEGIES FOR IMPROVEMENT

For research to inform practice, educators must begin to understand what strategies they can use within their building to improve performance. Measurement plays a critical role, but we also need to help educators understand this link between new indicators, their own classroom and school communities, and their role in shaping these indicators. Moving from a focus on the percentage of students who meet norms to a "value-added" approach changes one's perspective on student achievement away from external forces ("the kinds of kids I have") toward the classroom ("What do I do with the kids I have?"). Documenting that ninth grade attendance and grades are stronger predictors of graduating from high school than a student's incoming test scores and establishing that even higher-achieving students are vulnerable in this transition challenges educators to grapple with what is happening to students within their school rather than external factors beyond their control (e.g., students' prior achievement, or family and neighborhood forces).

Thus, researchers must provide critical evidence and rigorous frameworks that assist schools in focusing their improvement efforts. The concepts of social capital, relational trust, and program coherence help to organize data in ways that provide novel insight into problems. Thus, in Charles Lindblom's characterization, educators use data to solve the problem, moving quickly to solutions; in contrast, social scientists use the data to probe the problem, organize evidence to test theories and hypotheses, and look for anomalies. As illustrated in our example of program coherence, developing the key concepts provides a common language and focal point for educators in understanding their work and devising strategies for organizing efforts.

Assisting schools and the district in better understanding how to use indicators effectively has become a consistent role for CCSR. Recently, we helped the district and individual high schools understand the new high school testing system: the ACT Educational Planning and Assessment System (EPAS), which is comprised of EXPLORE, PLAN, and ACT. We were responding to the confusion and frustration that district staff and principals brought to CCSR as they struggled with how best to use the EPAS data to inform school improvement: "Can we look at student growth?" "Why are students doing so poorly on the ACT?" Our analysts began looking carefully at student performance differences across these tests and at the testing system itself. Our report entitled *From High School to the Future: ACT Preparation—Too Much, Too Late* analyzes students' performance and gains in performance in this testing system (Allensworth, Correa, Ponisciak, 2008). This report helps practitioners better understand their performance under this system and shifts the conversation away from test preparation to an analysis of the determinants of gains. This work also allows us to begin investigating which experiences in high school predict better-than-average growth in performance.

As illustrated in our on-track work, good measurement and indicator development also is critical to schools in identifying what they need to work on as they seek to improve long-term outcomes—what we term "leading indicators." Many schools that were concerned about dropout rates had adopted programs with little coherent vision of the critical predictors that were directly under the control of schools. On-track is a leading indicator that brings the big problem—reducing dropout rates—down to the day-to-day experiences of ninth grade students in the building. Similarly, one of the major findings of our EPAS analyses is that the students who show improvement (from EXPLORE to PLAN, and from PLAN to ACT) are those who do well in their courses (get high grades), regardless of their entering test scores. Thus, taking steps to strengthen student effort, increase student engagement, and ensure that students succeed in their courses should be the primary strategy that schools use to improve

ACT scores of students. This is a strategy few schools understood or engaged in as they struggled to improve scores and focused on the accountability demanded by the inclusion of the ACT into the state's testing system.

Our new research on the postsecondary outcomes of CPS students provides another example of this critical role. In 2005, CCSR began a unique partnership with CPS to track all their students into college or work. The first step was measurement. Our researchers worked closely with CPS staff to set up a valid tracking system that allowed us to understand what students' plans were on exiting CPS, compare those

Many schools concerned about dropout rates had adopted programs with little coherent vision of the critical predictors directly under schools' control. On-track is a leading indicator that brings the big problem—reducing dropout rates—down to the day-to-day experiences of ninth grade students in the building.

plans with actual enrollment, and track persistence and performance in college and work. A second step was to understand the determinants of those outcomes. In our first report, we focused specifically on trying to understand why, despite high aspirations, many CPS students were not making the transition to college and, when they did, were concentrated in two-year and non-selective colleges (Roderick et al., 2005). A major finding was that low ACT scores, and particularly low GPAs, constrained students' access. These findings challenged the approach that many principals initially followed in reacting to poor college attendance—delegating improvement efforts to the guidance department—and placed the central focus for raising college participation within the classroom. The report stimulated alignment of efforts to improve high school instruction with efforts to improve college readiness and access. Most important, it challenged educators to begin considering the role of student's course performance (GPAs) in shaping their college access. The findings changed the way the problem was conceptualized. Thus, whether postsecondary, on-track, or high stakes testing, our work has centered on helping principals, teachers, and the district understand how to organize their work to affect the indicators they decide to improve.

THEORY-DRIVEN EVALUATION: BUILDING NEW POLICY ON CUMULATIVE EXPERIENCE AND AVOIDING POLICY LURCH

Educational researchers must use rigorous methods (i.e., causal modeling and inference) to isolate the effects of particular practice and changes in policy to determine if investments in initiatives are effective. But in many cases, evaluation needs are more complex than isolating effects of an investment on one particular outcome or set of outcomes, and attempts to do this and make summative judgments about more general policy initiatives are often counterproductive. To start with, identifying the "treatment" can be complicated because most have multiple components and diverse effects. The policy to end social promotion is a good example. Did ending social promotion work? The theory of action was that the threat of retention would motivate students to work harder and produce incentives for adults to pay greater attention to children at risk. The initiative also put in place short-term supports, assuming that extra time on task would be an effective approach to help at-risk students catch up. Opponents of the policy argued that, even if there were benefits to some students, the policy relied on a practice—grade retention—that was harmful to all students.

> Painting complex stories is particularly critical for informing policy debates. It also is vital if research is to assist in building the capacity of systems to learn from the past and make corrections in the future....Theory-driven evaluation that paints complex pictures with evidence can contribute to policy development rather than dramatic policy lurch.

Evaluating the effect of ending social promotion meant setting out and testing this theory of action—weighing the evidence for effects, both positive and negative. Is there evidence that behavior was changed and that students were motivated and got more attention? Is there evidence that simply working harder and getting extra time on task was enough? Or, did teachers change their instructional practices? And, is there evidence that students who were retained suffered negative effects? Answering these questions required drawing on surveys, achievement data, and qualitative data. It required setting out and testing the basic thought process behind the policy, as well as investigating potential negative effects and unintended consequences. The result was not a definite yes or no; rather, it was a complex story of how the policy resolved some problems, revealed new problems, and had both positive and negative consequences. This constitutes theory-driven evaluation (Weiss, 1995, 1998).

Painting complex stories is particularly critical for informing policy debates. It also is vital if research is to assist in building the capacity of systems to learn from the past and make corrections in the future. Illuminating the "theory of action" behind the policy initiative, investigating whether and why proposed effects occurred, and understanding the consequences of programs and policies are essential if urban districts are to escape from the vicious cycle of enacting a policy, evaluating effects, concluding it doesn't work, discarding that approach, and enacting a disconnected new policy. Rather, theory-driven evaluation has the potential to allow the new policy to build on the potential benefits and lessons from the old policy.

Our recent work on evaluating small schools in Chicago demonstrated how theory-driven evaluation that paints complex pictures with evidence can contribute to policy development rather than dramatic policy lurch. In 2003, with support from the Gates Foundation and several local foundations, CPS began an ambitious initiative to break large high schools into smaller sub-units by creating new, freestanding small high schools. This effort, which was called the Chicago High School Redesign Initiative (CHRSI), represented one of the district's major high school reform strategies at the time. Our researchers, in collaboration with program developers, carefully laid out the theory of action that explained why these new small schools would obtain better student outcomes. Through our regular surveys and other data collection, the researchers measured most of the important components of the theory. Using a "real-time" and collaborative approach to this evaluation, we influenced many ongoing decisions. Most of these decisions pointed to the need for instructional improvements. This process required a new mode of work for us, with more frequent, brief reports produced with very quick turnaround. The research found that small schools did lead to greater personalization and higher engagement, manifest both through higher attendance and lower dropout rates. However, there was little evidence to show that the small schools led to greater achievement, at least as measured by test scores. These findings helped reformers in the city understand the limits of this structural approach to high school reform. Rather than simply judging the results a "failure," they developed subsequent reform strategies focusing on instructional improvements. Most importantly, the lesson from that experience and the CCSR research strongly shaped district approaches to opening new schools and reforming existing high schools. Thus, our engaged research led to refinement and development of specific policy, rather than a wholesale shift in approach.

Conclusion

There has traditionally been a divide in educational research between those who study policy development and governance structures that shape school reform on the national, state, and district level and those who study classroom practices, the details of instruction, and the work of teachers and principals. During the 1980s and 1990s, this disconnect also was prevalent in the ways policies were enacted versus what actually happened in classrooms. Researchers documented how many educational policy initiatives failed because educators "buffered" themselves from change, preventing major initiatives from accomplishing fundamental improvements in schools. The problem, researchers argued, was that educators on the front line had little incentive to change (Elmore, 1996; Payne, 2008). Principals had little discretion—essentially taking their charge from the central office, dealing with the teachers and students assigned to them, and having little expectation that they could drive instruction or move the performance of their students. Thus, educators had little incentive or authority to improve. The work of the classroom basically was divorced from large policy initiatives, and the work of the principal was to protect her teachers from the vicissitudes of central office policies and reform agendas. "Just wait, in time this will go away as the other initiatives have" was the standard response in the teachers' lounge to any announcement of a new program.

We would assert that this is not the world in which most teachers, principals, and school system administrators in large districts work today. Across the country (and especially in large urban districts), teachers, principals, and central office staff are under tremendous pressure to reform. Chicago heralded this new era when it de-centralized hiring, authority, and discretion over instructional programs to individual principals and schools in 1989. Under No Child Left Behind, and even prior to that, strong accountability initiatives in states and districts placed tremendous pressure on schools to reform. Many large school districts have come to believe that "the school is the unit of change"; therefore, they have adopted governance structures that devolve even greater authority to the school level.

Discerning the most crucial questions to investigate, building a cumulative knowledge base, and bringing findings to bear on local policy and practice all require focus on a single school district or geographic location. This is a radical departure from most scholarly research.

New schools and charters have introduced competition for students and teachers and created a group of R&D institutions that are expected to create new models and dramatically different outcomes in very short periods of time. Many of these changes were informed by earlier educational research. Standards promoted more tightly coupled systems in which it would be clear what students should learn, how this would be tested, and what the consequences were for schools if student performance lagged. The accountability movement sought to bring incentives to the school and classroom level by measuring outcomes that matter, to send strong signals to schools to focus on those outcomes, and to increase competition and the flow of information.

These changes have dramatically restructured the landscape of educational reform and, we would argue, made it even more important that research bridges the historical divide between the work of schools and the policies that govern them. Clearly, optimal education policy must assure that the big initiatives are linked to what matters most for improving performance. But, how can research address the disconnect between policy and practice? And, how best can research support schools in responding to these new opportunities and demands?

These are the questions that have guided CCSR researchers for almost 20 years. In this report, we have tried to present our answer to these questions. CCSR evolved as an organization by responding to changing demands and the complexity of educa-tion reform in a new era. The mission of CCSR is to support the search for solutions in ways that build the capacity of school reform and build coherence in identifying strategies and the levers for improvement across various levels of the district. Instead of asking whether reforms work, CCSR's research examines the critical factors that shape student achievement and the outcomes that schools are being asked to achieve. By using that approach, CCSR's research helps the school system and individual schools understand the outcomes that matter most and the processes within schools that may shape those outcomes, regardless of the particular reform program. This approach, we argue, supports coherence and focus at all levels of the system. Under the best scenario, schools should be measured on outcomes that matter (e.g., being on-track for ninth graders); district initiatives should be aligned to support schools' focus on those outcomes; and schools should be managing their efforts to improve those outcomes, based on extant research on the critical determinants of student success.

However, this approach also requires research support at all levels. The buzz phrase of the day is "data driven." Schools in many districts are increasingly being measured on an array of outcomes and are being expected to use data to assess their efforts and inform progress. In the absence of research supports, however, schools and districts struggle with the questions of what kinds of data to examine and how to use data to develop strategies for improvement. This is a gap CCSR has worked to fill. CCSR research supports the district in identifying the outcomes that they want to assess schools on, engages educators at all levels in understanding why those outcomes matter, and supports the development of strategies at both the school level and the district level.

Significantly, CCSR has demonstrated that it is not necessary to make tradeoffs between research quality, accessibility, and impact. Instead, high technical quality is critical if the research is to be believed and to produce cutting edge insights that can shape practice. It does mean, however, that research cannot rely on traditional means of disseminating research findings solely though publication and through technical peer-reviewed articles addressed to an academic audience. Rather, researchers must find new ways to engage the education community in research findings over time—through products that are accessible to a wide audience and through using diverse approaches that carefully attend to the process by which practitioners assimilate and internalize new information and connect it to their own problems.

Effectively supporting the search for solutions—what we term a new model for educational research that informs policy and practice—requires researchers to ask questions that address the core problems facing practitioners and decision makers and to see themselves less as "outside evaluators" and more as a resource that engages interactively with educators and reformers to build capacity for reform. Discerning the most crucial questions to investigate, building a cumulative knowledge base, and bringing findings to bear on local policy and practice all require focus on a single school district or geographic location. This is a radical departure from most scholarly research. Instead of becoming experts in testing, high school completion, school organization, and so forth, CCSR researchers combine expertise on a range of topics with knowledge of the Chicago Public Schools, the issues before them, and the larger set of factors that matter in improving them. The focus on one place allows the CCSR model to fully work.

This approach is a tall order for individual researchers, especially younger faculty members at universities who must meet expectations on peer publication and are subject to prevailing academic values. These values emphasize presentations at professional meetings and scholarly publications, rather than reports for public consumption and meetings with stakeholders. Furthermore, the professional relationships of academics tend not to lead them to work with local actors. Instead, faculty members are more likely to interact with colleagues around the country who may be working on the same problem (Bryk and Sebring, 2001).

Creating new models of research, then, ultimately means that new institutions need to support this work. We would argue that the challenge that CCSR poses to the research community is not about changing the role of an individual researcher but about creating a new role for universities in supporting school reform. As we have

> Ultimately the success of the model is not whether individual researchers produce a good piece of research, but whether specific research findings translate into policy and practice and contribute to the larger dialogue about what it will take to improve.

argued throughout this report, the work of CCSR is not about an individual researcher doing a good piece of research. We hypothesize that if each CCSR study had been conducted by an independent researcher who was working alone, our impact would have been minimal. Rather, we hope we have demonstrated how CCSR has worked to break down the silos, produce research findings, and then build on those findings by institutionalizing them into the education debate and ongoing research effort. Ultimately the success of the model is not whether individual researchers produce a good piece of research, but whether specific research findings translate into policy and practice and contribute to the larger dialogue about what it will take to improve. This also has meant changing the relationship between research and practice, so that the education community sees research not as external to reform but as a resource that facilitates ongoing development. This requires developing different sets of professional priorities and different sets of professional relationships for researchers than is currently available in traditional academic departments and research centers. It requires that universities promote and reward new models for research, ultimately creating new roles for universities in supporting their urban communities.

References

Allensworth, Elaine M., Macarena Correa, and Stephen Ponisciak (2008)
From High School to the Future: ACT Preparation—Too Much, Too Late. Chicago: Consortium on Chicago School Research at the University of Chicago.

Allensworth, Elaine M., and John Q. Easton (2007)
What Matters for Staying On-Track and Graduating in Chicago Public High Schools. Chicago: Consortium on Chicago School Research at the University of Chicago.

Allensworth, Elaine M., and John Q. Easton (2005)
The On-Track Indicator as a Predictor of High School Graduation. Chicago: Consortium on Chicago School Research at the University of Chicago.

Allensworth, Elaine M., Takako Nomi, Nick Montgomery, and Valerie Lee (2007)
"College preparatory curriculum for all in Chicago high schools: Consequences of ninth grade course taking on academic outcomes." (Manuscript submitted for publication.)

Balfanz, Robert, and Lettie Legters (2004)
Locating the Dropout Crisis: Which High Schools Produce the Nation's Dropouts? Where Are They Located? Who Attends Them? (Report 70) Baltimore, MD: Center for Research on the Education of Students Placed at Risk, Johns Hopkins University.

Balfanz, Robert, and Lettie Legters (2006)
The graduation rate crisis we know and what can be done about it? *Education Week*, (25) 42.

Bryk, Anthony S., and Barbara Schneider (2002)
Trust in Schools: A Core Resource for Improvement. New York: Russell Sage Foundation.

Bryk, Anthony S., and Penny B. Sebring (2001)
Informing Reform: The Work of the Consortium on Chicago School Research. Unpublished. Chicago: Consortium on Chicago School Research at the University of Chicago.

Bryk, Anthony S., Penny B. Sebring, David Kerbow, Sharon Rollow, and John Q. Easton (1998)
Charting Chicago School Reform: Democratic Localism as a Lever for Change. Boulder, CO: Westview Press.

Bryk, Anthony S., Yeow Meng Thum, John Q. Easton, and Stuart Luppescu (1998)
Academic Productivity of Chicago Public Elementary Schools. Chicago: Consortium on Chicago School Research at the University of Chicago.

Bryk, Anthony S., John Q. Easton, David Kerbow, Sharon Rollow, and Penny B. Sebring (1993)
A View from the Elementary Schools: The State of Reform in Chicago. Chicago: Consortium on Chicago School Research at the University of Chicago.

Dewey, John (1927)
The Public and its Problems. Troy, MO: Holt, Rinehart & Winston.

Easterly, William (2006)
The White Man's Burden: Why the West's Efforts to Aid the Rest have Done So Much Ill and So Little Good. New York: Penguin Press.

Elmore, Richard F. (1996)
Getting to scale with good educational practice. *Harvard Educational Review*, 66 (1), 1–26.

Finnigan, Kara, and Jennifer O'Day (2003)
External Support to Schools on Probation: Getting a Leg Up? Chicago: Consortium on Chicago School Research at the University of Chicago and University of Pennsylvania Consortium for Policy Research in Education.

Hess, G. Alfred, and Solomon Cytrynbaum (2002)
The effort to redesign Chicago High Schools: Effects on schools and achievement. In Valerie E. Lee (Ed.) *Reforming Chicago's High Schools: Research Perspectives on School and System Level Change.* Chicago, IL: Consortium on Chicago School Research at the University of Chicago.

Lindblom, Charles E., and David Cohen (1979)
Usable Knowledge: Social Science and Social Problem Solving. New Haven, CT: Yale University Press.

Lindblom, Charles E. (1990)
Inquiry and Change: The Troubled Attempt to Understand and Shape Society. New Haven, CT: Yale University Press.

References

Miller, Shazia, Elaine M. Allensworth, and Julie Kochanek (2002)
Student Performance: Course Taking, Test Scores, and Outcomes. Chicago: Consortium on Chicago School Research at the University of Chicago.

Nagaoka, Jenny, and Melissa Roderick (2004)
Ending Social Promotion in Chicago: The Academic Progress of Retained Students. Chicago: Consortium on Chicago School Research at the University of Chicago.

Newmann, Fred M., Gudelia Lopez, and Anthony S. Bryk (1998)
The Quality of Intellectual Work in Chicago Schools: A Baseline Report. Chicago: Consortium on Chicago School Research at the University of Chicago.

Newmann, Fred M., BetsAnn Smith, Elaine M. Allensworth, and Anthony S. Bryk (2001)
School Instructional Coherence: Benefits and Challenges. Chicago: Consortium on Chicago School Research at the University of Chicago.

Roderick, Melissa, Anthony S. Bryk, Brian Jacob, John Q. Easton, and Elaine M. Allensworth (1999)
Ending Social Promotion in Chicago: Results from the First Two Years. Chicago: Consortium on Chicago School Research at the University of Chicago.

Roderick, Melissa, and Eric Camburn (1996)
Academic difficulty during the high school transition. Section III in Penny Bender Sebring, Anthony S. Bryk, Melissa Roderick, and Eric Camburn (authors) *Charting Reform in Chicago: The Students Speak.* Chicago: Consortium on Chicago School Research at the University of Chicago.

Roderick, Melissa, and Eric Camburn (1999)
Risk and recovery from course failure in the early years of high school. *American Educational Research Journal,* (36) 2, 303–44.

Roderick, Melissa, Miriam Engel, Jenny Nagaoka, and Brian Jacob (2003)
Ending Social Promotion in Chicago: Results from Summer Bridge. Chicago: Consortium on Chicago School Research at the University of Chicago.

Roderick, Melissa, Jenny Nagaoka, and Elaine M. Allensworth (2005)
Is the glass half full or mostly empty? Ending social promotion in Chicago in Edward H. Haertel and Joan Herman (Eds.) *Uses and Misuses of Data for Educational Accountability and Improvement,* The 104th Yearbook for the National Society for the Study of Education (NSSE), Part 2, 223–59. Malden, MA: National Society for the Study of Education.

Roderick, Melissa, Jenny Nagaoka, Vanessa Coca, and Eliza Moeller (2008)
From High School to the Future: Potholes on the Road to College. Chicago: Consortium on Chicago School Research at the University of Chicago.

Roderick, Melissa, Jenny Nagaoka, Elaine M. Allensworth, Vanessa Coca, Macarena Correa, and Ginger Stoker (2006)
From High School to The Future: A First Look at Chicago Public School Graduates' College Enrollment, College Preparation, and Graduation from Four-Year Colleges. Chicago: Consortium on Chicago School Research at the University of Chicago.

Sebring, Penny, Anthony Bryk, Melissa Roderick, Eric Camburn, Stuart Luppescu, Yeow Meng Thum, BetsAnn Smith, and Joseph Kahne (1996)
Charting Reform in Chicago: The Students Speak. Chicago: Consortium on Chicago School Research at the University of Chicago.

Smith, BetsAnn (1998)
It's About Time: Opportunities to Learn. Chicago: Consortium on Chicago School Research at the University of Chicago.

Sporte, Susan, and Joseph Kahne (2007)
Educating for Democracy: Lessons from Chicago. Chicago: Consortium on Chicago School Research at the University of Chicago.

Stevens, David (2008)
If Small Is Not Enough . . .? The Characteristics of Successful Small High Schools in Chicago. Chicago: Consortium on Chicago School Research at the University of Chicago.

Endnotes

Swanson, Christopher B. (2004)
*The Real Truth about Low Graduation Rates:
An Evidence-Based Commentary.*
Washington DC: The Urban Institute.

United States National Commission on Excellence
in Education (1983)
*A Nation at Risk: The Imperative for Educational
Reform. A Report to the Nation and the Secretary
of Education, United States Department of
Education by the National Commission on
Excellence in Education.*

Wagner, Peter, Carol H. Weiss, Bjyrn Wittrock,
and Hellmut Wollman (1991)
*Social Sciences and Modern States: National
Experiences and Theoretical Crossroads
(advances in political science).* New York:
Cambridge University Press.

Weiss, Carol H. (1995)
Nothing as practical as good theory:
Exploring theory-based evaluation for
comprehensive community initiatives
for children and families. In J. P. Connell,
A. C. Kubisch, L. B. Schorr, and C. H.
Weiss (Eds.), *New Approaches to Evaluating
Community Initiatives: Concepts, Methods, and
Contexts,* 65–92. Aspen, CO: Roundtable on
Comprehensive Community Initiatives for
Children and Families.

Weiss, Carol H. (1998)
*Evaluation: Methods for Studying Programs
and Policies.* Second Edition. New Jersey:
Prentice Hall.

Weiss, Carol H. (1991)
*Organizations for Policy Analysis: Helping
Government Think.* Thousand Oaks, CA:
Sage Publications.

Weiss, Carol H., and Michael J. Bucuvalas (1980)
Social Science Research and Decision-Making.
New York: Columbia University Press.

1 William Easterly (2006) used the term "search for solutions" to characterize an alternative model to policy planning in development.

2 This finding, that the technical quality of a study was a significant contributor to decision makers' assessment of its usefulness, actually contradicted the assessments that Weiss and Bucuvalas obtained from the social scientists. They found that social scientists thought that technical quality would make only a marginal difference in the views of decisions makers.

About the Authors

Melissa Roderick

Melissa Roderick is the Principal Investigator of the Chicago Postsecondary Transition Project. She is the Hermon Dunlap Smith Professor at the School of Social Service Administration at the University of Chicago and a co-director at CCSR. Professor Roderick is an expert in urban school reform, high-stakes testing, minority adolescent development, and school transitions.

John Q. Easton

John Q. Easton is Executive Director of the Consortium on Chicago School Research. He has been affiliated with CCSR since its inception in 1990 and led its first research study. Much of Easton's research at CCSR examines trends in achievement test scores and the use of test scores in school improvement and school accountability efforts. He is coauthor of a recent study on the relationship between freshman-year academic performance and high school graduation. Easton holds a PhD in Measurement, Evaluation, and Statistical Analysis from the University of Chicago.

Penny Bender Sebring

Penny Bender Sebring is a Founding Co-Director of CCSR. She is lead author of the report, *The Essential Supports for School Improvement* (2006). Sebring received a BA in sociology from Grinnell College, where she is a Life Trustee. She received a PhD in education and policy studies from Northwestern University. She serves on the board of directors for the Chicago Public Education Fund.

This report reflects the interpretation of the authors. Although the Consortium's Steering Committee provided technical advice and reviewed earlier versions, no formal endorsement by these individuals, organizations, or the full Consortium should be assumed.

This report was produced by the Consortium's publications and communications staff.

Editing and project management by Publications & Creative Services
Graphic design by Jeff Hall Design

02-09/1M/CSR09196

Consortium on Chicago School Research

Our Mission

The Consortium on Chicago School Research (CCSR) at the University of Chicago conducts research of high technical quality that can inform and assess policy and practice in the Chicago Public Schools. We seek to expand communication among researchers, policy makers, and practitioners as we support the search for solutions to the problems of school reform. CCSR encourages the use of research in policy action and improvement of practice, but does not argue for particular policies or programs. Rather, we help to build capacity for school reform by identifying what matters for student success and school improvement, creating critical indicators to chart progress, and conducting theory-driven evaluation to identify how programs and policies are working.

www.ingramcontent.com/pod-product-compliance
Lightning Source LLC
Chambersburg PA
CBHW041427090426
42741CB00002B/72